# Top of the Class Teacher Interviews

## 55 Power-Packed Strategies to Maximize Preparation and Supercharge Your Confidence

David M. Rische

Foreword by Ken McGuire

Please visit my site for inspiration, encouragement, and learning, at:

www.davidrische.com

ISBN 13: 978-1974560684
ISBN-10: 1974560686

# DEDICATION

This book is dedicated to all the educators who: Encourage and believe in your students every day, speak life, embrace creativity, spend your own money for their needs, go to their games and performances, cast visions of hope, lose sleep over them, are not swayed by the latest discouraging legislature, believe and live out that every child can learn, and are fueled with passion and persistence. You know who you are – but because of your character, you keep it quiet.

# CONTENTS

## 2. The External Prep Phase                                    16

# FOREWORD

Great leaders and managers know that in order for their school or business to succeed at the highest levels, they must hire and surround themselves with outstanding talent. Likewise, talented applicants know that for them to grow and express their potential – they must work in an environment that fits and strengthens their skills and abilities. In the following work, David Rische draws on his years as a highly successful school principal. He also takes from his hours of intentional leadership, and a variety of talent identification trainings. His goal is to provide readers with the insights and techniques to participate in the preparation and reflection process towards a successful interview.

My association with David has afforded me the opportunity to witness his schools flourish and become high achieving communities of learning. As he masterfully assembles and develops a team of professionals - the school culture is strengthened, instructional expertise grows, and student performance increases. Ultimately, the winners are the students.

Grasping these concepts will enable the reader to present themselves professionally and personally in a high quality interview setting. Good luck!

Ken McGuire
Educational Leader
Retired International Leadership Consultant

# INTRODUCTION

Point number one: this book does not guarantee that you will obtain a teaching job.

However, if you actively apply the strategies shared – your chances tremendously increase. The principles put into action will make you better at the interview process.

Point number two: Are you sure you want to get into the teaching business?

You are signing up for a career that . . . .

*Will test you physically and emotionally.*
*Will have you missing some of your own children's events because of your commitment to attend functions at your school.*
*Will have you grading papers and planning late at night.*
*Will shock you by what comes out of young people's mouths.*
*Will provide you with a mixture of all abilities in your classroom.*

However, you are also signing up for a career that can literally change the world by investing yourself into the lives of students.

Upon reflection, a squadron of teachers come to mind that impacted my life:

*My dad who taught at a private school for an extremely low salary. He coached three sports and didn't receive a dime extra in pay. It was more important for a group of young boys to have the experience of playing team sports. And I would often see him spending his own money to purchase equipment for us.*

*The seventh grade teacher that told me she took my creative writing home and read it to her family for laughs. Might that have something to do with me enjoying writing now?*

*The high school English teacher that encouraged me to try out for the school play and gave me funny parts. Might that have something to do with me being a ham on stage now?*

*The football coach that stopped by my house and dropped off a set of weights and a bench for me for free. He helped a scrawny kid filled with doubts build confidence and a love for exercise.*

*The college professor that first introduced me to the Socratic Method for teaching a class. He took the potentially dry subject of Business Law and made it my favorite.*

*And finally, the crazy "Pirate Guy" from San Diego that helped me rediscover my childhood love for magic at the age of 49.*

Many others came along my path that helped me get from Point A to Point B in my life's journey. What about you? It is a beneficial exercise to think back on each teacher you had and how they transformed your life. I could also take time to highlight the rotten apples that had a negative impact on me – but I want to keep this uplifting.

Point number three: My perspective may be completely different from other principals. However, one of my main goals for the reader is to see through the eyes of someone who has sat through hundreds, if not thousands of interviews - and recommended for hire hundreds of employees.

Instead of multiple searches on the Internet, this book can be a resource or a "one stop shop" to guide you into the preparation you need. Yes, by all means – use the internet to stay current and as a supplement. You can have peace of mind knowing these strategies are from someone sharing from experience compared to an unknown contributor on the World Wide Web. Some of the strategies cut to the chase and are extremely short. Others are more intricately detailed and are several pages long.

This book is divided into six sections or phases. First, *The Research Phase* is your starting point in self-reflection regarding the teacher job. Do you have the internal (heart) and external (paperwork) qualities to take on this challenging and yet fulfilling career?

Second, *The External Prep Phase* serves as a checklist as you finalize your application for a specific teaching job. Discover what makes an eye-catching application, cover letter, resume, and portfolio. What if the committee asks you to give a demonstration lesson?

Third, *The Internal Prep Phase* focuses on the incredibly important mental preparation that goes on before the interview. How to build a positive mindset, what to look out for, and some small tips designed to strengthen your confidence before you start answering questions.

Fourth, *The Waiting Area Phase* breaks down your mental preparation even further. Those key moments right before entering the interview room. Showing warmth and friendliness to the office staff, taking a detailed look at all your surroundings while you wait, and borrowing a technique from The Navy Seals to help you calm down.

Fifth, *The Interview Phase* is a section with absolutely nothing in it. Because you are creating this portion while you interview. This is where all of your hard work and preparation can finally be implemented. No one knows what is going to go on behind the closed door – you are writing this section in real time.

Finally, section six is *The Remember and Reflection* Phase. The focus here is on what to do after the interview. However, some of the strategies you would obviously think about and apply before and during the interview. Logistically – I wanted them to be grouped with the strategies that focus on the conclusion of the interview and the days that follow. Reflection is always a powerful tool if we use it to learn and progress forward, versus zeroing in on what went wrong and becoming stuck in self-condemning beliefs about ourselves.

You may be able to tell by the brief description of each phase that the majority of this book is about preparation. It is incredibly disheartening for anyone giving an interview to have a candidate in front of them that is fully qualified, but cannot present themselves in an effective way during the questioning portions. Even worse is the candidate with qualifications and experiences, but showed up unprepared for the interview. Good news - being nervous for an interview is 100% normal. The strategies applied in this book can help you lower the intensity level of your nervousness. I would like to promise complete elimination of anxiety, but I can't. A comparison can be made to purchasing a gym membership – but staying home on the couch binge watching shows, and still hoping you'll get in shape. Reading and thinking about these strategies will help, but with many of them you must take some steps of action. More good news is that – sometimes the action steps are incredibly small. That could be the driving force that makes you 1% different than someone else applying for the same job.

This book was primarily written for brand new teacher candidates, or teachers with experience attempting to change positions or reenter the workforce. However, a significant portion of the research discovered was from the business world. I believe that anyone wanting to brush up on their interview skills or receive additional insight can benefit from reading this. It may even help those giving and participating in the interview process as a checklist or refresher.

Some readers may want to pour through the text cover to cover. Great! Others may just want to read about the strategies relevant to them or those that peak their interests. Perfect! Maybe there is an area or areas of struggle during interviews that you just can't seem to conquer – hopefully this book touches on that area in some way that will give you a new perspective and hope.

Concluding, my goal is that this book remains relevant for years to come. You may need immediate help for an interview coming up in a few days. Or, you might not participate in an interview for the next 5 to 10 years. Either way, this can be a timeless resource that has the potential to strengthen your confidence at any point during your career journey.

Kids are facing challenges like never before. In my opinion, they need top-notch, wheels-off, wildly creative, loving, over-the-top teachers now more than ever. They don't need rotten apples that will intensify their cynicism, negativity, and increase their boredom in school. If you have the skill set, creativity, can get along with other adults, some organization skills, a willingness to keep learning, and love of children (somewhere between PreK and High School) – there is a teaching position somewhere for you. Use and implement these strategies to help get you there faster.

# THE RESEARCH PHASE

*It's the 'hard' that makes it great. Otherwise, everybody would be doing it.*

- **Tom Hanks**

1

# STRATEGY 1: THE NUMBER ONE QUALITY YOU CAN'T FAKE

*Education World* published an article titled "What Qualities Do Principals Look For in a New Teacher?" The answer was . . . passion. Passion is the key. If there's one word that was repeated over and over by principals, it was the word passion. Passion for knowledge. Passion for teaching. Passion for kids.[1]

Take a look deep inside and ask: What am I passionate about? What gets me excited and enthused? What do I love doing and I lose all track of time?

The next item to ponder is: Where can I teach that subject or something similar?

A challenge you will face is: How are you going to convince the interview panel that you have passion without saying, "I have passion" a dozen times?

You can fake a lot of things, but you can't fake passion. You can be taught content, subjects, classroom management, and best instructional practices. You can't teach passion. And you will need iron-clad passion to help you persevere when you inevitably ask, "Now why did I get into teaching?" Because passion can only take you so far as we see in Strategy 2 . . .

# STRATEGY 2: THE SECOND QUALITY YOU CAN'T FAKE

Truly wanting to work with kids. All kinds. An internal belief that all of them can learn and be successful. Preferences are fine – older, younger, special needs, or gifted. However, you must be prepared for a wide mosaic of students no matter what age group you are hired for. Because they will test you, make you proud, push you, impress you, and frustrate you. Delight in your subject matter can only get you so far. You must also be passionate about reaching every kid that walks through your classroom door. You have to have the mindset that you are going to love the unlovable. Because they aren't going to sit in rows and allow you to lecture all day without any interruptions. And they aren't going to immediately absorb your content matter and ace every assignment you give them.

This can be spotted several different ways during an interview. Eyes brightening, widening, or tearing up. Smiling while talking and a candidates voice speeding up. Success stories on not giving up on a kid. Also stories of heavily investing in a young person – and unfortunately they end up making unwise decisions.

You can love your subject – but you have to love kids also. Otherwise, you'll be ineffective and think, "Well, no one warned me kids would act this way." You're being warned now.

There is nothing wrong with only wanting to teach a certain age group – each one has its advantages and disadvantages. You can't be all things to all people. Do you really want to apply for every opening prekindergarten through high school that a district has to offer? What conclusions might the hiring committee draw when they see that? Most job opening databases feature the function of showing a person's application history. Proceed with wisdom and caution.

Each age group is a true calling. So take a deep look inside before you apply.

For preschool, you will need unending patience, outrageous amounts of energy, and the willingness to act silly every now and then. Elementary teachers are qualified to teach all subject areas, but need to be exceptionally strong at teaching reading. Reading is the key to academic success, and literacy is stressed in every elementary school. In order to teach students in the middle grades, you need to be a little like an elementary teacher and a little like a high school teacher. In other words, you need to like children/young adolescents, and you need to be a subject-matter specialist. And finally, high school teachers consider themselves subject-matter experts and often report that they chose teaching because they love their subjects. High school teachers like to inspire teenagers/young adults to learn all there is to know about a subject.[2]

One final thought – it is okay to switch subjects and age preferences. I started out my teaching certification program as a P.E. major wanting to coach football at the high school level. I ended up obtaining a Master's degree as a Reading Specialist and getting my first job as a third grade teacher for all subjects. Throughout my teaching career, I discovered that my "sweet spot" was teaching fifth grade mathematics and science. At the time of this writing, I'm an administrator at a Prekindergarten Learning Center. Go figure.

# STRATEGY 3: WHERE DO I START THIS JOURNEY?

Besides online searches, the certification program at the university you are attending should be able to give you some leads. C'mon, that's the reason you went there and paid the big bucks. Campuses usually have some type of job center or student posting center. Alternative certification programs have a system they implement to help their students find jobs. District websites are a great resource, you just need to keep a close watch if a position posted is outdated.

As much as possible, participate in any and all job fairs. I have found some tremendous candidates at job fairs that either I or someone else hired. The fairs offer you a great opportunity to practice an incredibly quick summarization of why you are the perfect candidate the district is looking for. Think far in advance how you are going to differentiate yourself from the hundreds, if not thousands of applicants there. Remember, it is a conversation – not a monologue. Typically you'll have thirty seconds to one minute to state your case. A line will be forming behind you, or the district representatives may have business to attend to. Sometimes, they may ask you for an interview right on the spot. Or, they might be collecting resumes – so don't come empty handed.

Like every other job you might apply for one major rule applies – do you know anyone in the system? Another disclaimer, just because you know someone does not mean you have a smooth path to being hired.

When people hint to me not so subtly, "Hey, guess who is going to have their teaching certification next year???" My response is always the same: "That's great! If anything, I can possibly promise you an interview opportunity at my school if you apply for open positions, and are qualified. However, I CAN NOT promise you a job."

# STRATEGY 4:  HOW'S YOUR PAPER TRAIL?

Unfortunately, candidates don't always read the certification requirements for the job in which they are applying. Especially if you have certification from another state. A librarian certification from Florida probably won't get you the middle school head volleyball coach position in Wyoming you just submitted an electronic application for. Check with your state education agency to see where you stand. Discover what credits will transfer from another state, and what gaps you need to take care of in your certification. It also good to contact the Human Resources Department just to double check, and that you have a clear understanding of what you need and the timeline involved. See what you can do as quickly as possible to get certified for the state or for particular job you desire. Frequently you can take a test instead of going through the long process of taking classes and obtaining credits. A hiring team can still hire you if your status is "pending" or "anticipated". Particularly if you are applying for a hard to fill position. However, the person ready to go already has an advantage over you – especially if a school needs to fill a position quickly.

# STRATEGY 5: DO YOU KNOW WHERE YOU'RE GOING?

No - not geographically you silly! Do you know unique details about the school you're applying at? "Insider information" that you obtained from the campus or district website, personal experiences, or quality dialogue (not gossip). Do you know about the community that surrounds the school? It is impressive when a candidate makes comments like:

"I saw on your website the upcoming Fun Run . . ."
"When I looked at the state report on your campus demographics I noticed the trend of . . ."
"I discovered that you have a chess club after school – I would love to be a part of that, or even expand it to a game club."

This shows the candidate did their homework. Spend some quality time researching the school or schools you are applying at. Take notes of 2 -3 things that makes that school special, or items you can use as talking points during the interview. You may even uncover some challenges that stand out in the data. Perfect opportunity to share concrete examples how you, your skill set, and your past experiences can help improve those challenges.

# STRATEGY 6: DID YOU EVEN READ THE JOB DESCRIPTION?

Or, are you one of those individuals that applies for every open position a school district has? Frequently, a hiring committee will sort through stacks of resumes or databases, and think they have found a great prospective candidate to interview. It is a waste of everyone's time when the person being interviewed acts surprised when certain duties are mentioned. Many special education or prekindergarten positions require a willingness to take care of students' toileting needs. "Other duties as assigned" is code for evening events, arrival and dismissal duty, and being available for meetings or trainings. Depending on the age, "maintaining emotional composure under stress" comes into play if a child curses, hits, spits, or storms out of your class in a tirade. Read the description carefully. Know what you're signing up for.

When you are first starting out with a teaching job, you will not be able to be the last one to arrive in the mornings and the first one to leave right after student dismissal. Teams or administrators may need to meet. Parents may only be available for a conference at 5 pm. Your school will need you to volunteer at evening events. Your principal might lead long-winded faculty meetings. You must be flexible before becoming a teacher.

# STRATEGY 7: VOLUNTEER ALL OVER THE PLACE

A great opportunity to obtain insight into a school is to sign up as a volunteer. Attend events that are open to the community like sporting events, performances, and parent/community organizations.

If your schedule or location won't allow you direct access to the schools you are interested in, engage in anything else that gives you quality experiences working with kids: babysitting, nanny, coaching, Boys and Girls Scouts, teaching Sunday School, Vacation Bible School, YMCA, and Summer Camps.

Even community volunteering at hospitals, nursing homes, and libraries shows that you have a compassionate heart and character regarding the needs of others.

Besides strengthening your resume, all these varied experiences will more than likely resurface sometime during your teaching career to assist you in ways you had not envisioned.

# STRATEGY 8: WHAT ARE YOU READING BESIDES *HARRY POTTER?*

Fiction is great – especially if you are keeping up with what young people are reading. Former president Theodore Roosevelt has been given credit for the quote, "Leaders are Readers." As a teacher, you are a leader. You will have influence, impact, and the opportunity to change the trajectory of lives. Why not learn from the best? A $20 investment or a free trip to the library can help you tap into the minds and techniques of master teachers, educators, and leaders.

Passion was mentioned earlier – but life-long learning and continuous improvement need to be in the mixture if you are going to teach. Great educators crave knowledge they can use to transform their classrooms. Those same individuals also welcome constructive criticism because they want the best for their students. Those with a growth mindset have an attitude of humility that they "haven't arrived", and keep that attitude throughout their careers.

You should also be able to articulate a brief understanding of the latest trends, best practices, and legislative updates in the vast realm of education. Plus, have a strong knowledge of the ever-increasing world of education jargon and acronyms. It sometimes feels like speaking a second language.

Even if it is a magazine article or a post on the internet – be prepared to discuss in an interview how you are improving yourself, staying updated, and continuing your education while you are waiting to be hired. Being well read is a significant key to success in any endeavor you are pursuing.

# STRATEGY 9:  BIG BROTHER IS WATCHING YOU

The probability is high that the hiring committee will do an online search of your name before or after the interview. The majority of interview articles I read from the business world said that this is standard practice now. Clean up your posts once you start applying to school districts. Although hilarious, that picture of you with the lampshade on your head at the New Year's Party has got to go. Try typing in your name into a search engine and see what appears.

Whether you agree with it or not, you will be held to a higher standard as a public educator. Even on your select "private" accounts – once something is out there, it is out there. Think about, what if your postings were the headline on a newspaper or website?

Personal opinion - I would be cautious in having parents and especially students as your followers on personal accounts. To provide an option for social media, many school employees create accounts for their classroom or campus. And they also set a filter so someone in charge can control what gets approved to go on the site.

Over two decades ago when I applied at a certain district – they contacted me that someone with a criminal record was using my name as an alias! These days were pre-cell phone, pre-internet, and pre-social media. Fortunately, they were able to clear my name and I ended up getting hired. So be extra careful and cautious in making sure your name has nothing negative attached to it.

# STRATEGY 10: CHART YOUR BELIEFS AND EXPERIENCES

A former supervisor gave me this advice as I was preparing for an interview to hopefully move from Assistant Principal to Principal. This is a strategy to help you shape your beliefs and philosophies regarding the teaching field. It may also help jog your memory of past experiences that you have had working with young people. It could also provide an outlet for you to record new learning that you have recently encountered. And finally, it is a visual tool – a memory of what you wrote down may come to mind right in the middle of your interview when you are desperately grasping for an answer.

To start, find a quiet place and block out about 30 – 60 minutes. On sheet of paper, horizontally write down key categories for the teaching job you are interested in. For example: Classroom Management, Differentiation, Gifted Students, Special Needs Students, Technology Integration, Creative Hooks, and specific content areas. Then, just let your mind flow freely as you write down what comes to mind regarding these classifications. Additional categories may come to mind during this process. You'll be surprised at how much you write down. Or, you may not have ever seriously thought about: What is my philosophy/experiences regarding _____?

A day or two before your interview, take a look at this chart to help build a little bit extra mental muscle in your preparation work.

# STRATEGY 11: IDENTIFY GAPS IN YOUR TEACHER PREPARATION PROGRAM

I have no issues regarding the certification program I went through to become a teacher. However, once I experienced my first year as a teacher – I realized I was completely unprepared in three areas. Those are: classroom management, special education, and how to communicate effectively with parents.

Regarding *classroom management*, I was not ready the first time a student told me to "shut up". My mental image of my first class was of me flawlessly presenting the subjects to students with bright eyes hanging on the edge of their seats at my every word. Then, I would seamlessly hand out a worksheet or two to fully validate my instructional prowess. They would sit quietly working, and then read a book until we were ready to progress to the next subject when I would repeat the exact same format. You can see why a frustrated student told me to shut up.

Fortunately, I had a strong mentor teacher to observe. Classroom management was her strength. It was on the job training for me. I was continually trying new techniques and methods to find out what motivated the kids and how to keep them engaged. Some worked, some were okay, and some completely bombed. I also tried to read every book about classroom discipline systems that I could get my hands on. My greatest discovery was the power of building relationships with the students. Taking a sincere interest in who they were and what they were interested in. My second greatest discovery was the effectiveness of positive language, positive motivation, and positive incentives instead of a punishment mentality. Sometimes it takes an incredible amount of time to discover – but I believe every child has something that can serve as a motivator. Another challenge, is that sometimes that motivator is a moving target and frequently changes. Read up, get experiences with classrooms, camps, or volunteering with children at church. Have a system in place mentally or from experience before you step into the interview room. I can't

13

emphasize enough – if you can't manage the students – the odds are incredibly high that you won't last as a teacher.

The second area was *special education*. In my certification program we learned about disabilities and modifying the curriculum so all students can experience success. However, I did not know anything about ARD meetings until I sat in my first one. Some states call them IEP meetings, or even have other titles. It is the meeting to decide whether a student needs special education services, a review of their current services, or if can they be dismissed from special education. These meetings feature specialists, parents, an administrator, teachers, and sometimes professionals or legal advocates. These meetings are a big deal. Everyone is legally bound to what is decided in that meeting. You are helping determine the future path of a student in hopes of giving them all the support they need regarding their particular disability. Whatever state you are in, study up on the multitude of acronyms surrounding special education, what their meetings are called, and what is the teacher's responsibility in that meeting. One teacher shared with me that in her previous state – the teachers were in charge of all the preliminary testing of the student and they basically ran the meeting instead of a specialist. In the interview, you don't want to have a blank stare and reply with an "I don't know" when asked a question about special education.

The third area was *dealing with parents*, especially when they are angry. This is a tricky area, because it is unpredictable when it will occur and what the topic will be. Many challenges or disputes with parents end up having the root cause being something to do with communication. You always want to be proactive with the communication in your class. Unfortunately, someone is going to be upset with you at some point. One way to prepare for this is to reflect on conflict you have had in the past. It could be with a co-worker, a supervisor, a teen-ager, a spouse or significant other, an in-law or outlaw – the possibilities are endless. How did you confront the situation? Did you remain calm? Were you seeking to understand their side, or completely focused on what your next line was going to be? What was the end result? Were you striving for a "win-win" outcome? The skills you've used in the past will be a great predictor of how you will act in the future when conflict arises. This is one area you will continue to learn and grow in your entire career. I would strongly recommend *Dealing With Difficult Parents* by Todd Whitaker for a holistic view of where parents are coming from –

and the skills and strategies to help you prosper through the most challenging interactions with parents or guardians. There are also numerous books and articles available regarding the subject of successfully navigating through difficult conversations.

Bonus advice: Join a professional organization as soon as membership opens up. That will serve as protection for you if you are unjustly or falsely accused during your career – especially in the three areas mentioned above.

# THE EXTERNAL PREP PHASE

*Between the dream's inspiration and its manifestation, there's going to be lots of perspiration.*

**- Jon Maxwell**

# STRATEGY 12: PUT SOME EFFORT INTO THE APPLICATION PROCESS

There is a fine balance between submitting a quality application and taking forever to make it perfect. Every day it is not sent - in you could be losing valuable ground for the perfect teaching position. Procrastination will be screaming out your name wanting to be best friends.

After each section, read your writing out loud to hear any errors. Ask a family member, friend, or co-worker to proof read before submitting. Barter with them their favorite cup of coffee or a lunch beyond fast food.

Many districts include a video interview as part of the complete application package. Embrace the opportunity! Look nice, but don't wear a prom dress or tuxedo. Find a comfortable place where you can be relaxed giving the answers, especially if they are timed. If a cat, dog, or child unexpectedly runs in the background – show you have a sense of humor by being able to laugh it off and quickly resolve it. Figure out how you are going to show warmth, positivity, and a smile – without acting like you are auditioning for a role as one of the cast members at Disneyland. If you can't smile at all during the entire video interview – what does that say about the kind of person who will be greeting children or teenagers every day?

# STRATEGY 13: THIS IS NOT THE TIME FOR YOUR AUTOBIOGRAPHY

This was hinted in Strategy 12. I've witnessed both extremes in reviewing applications. A complete rush job where the applicant is obviously in a hurry to turn everything in. Brief, one sentence responses with little to no substance in them. Typos, grammatical errors, and outdated information are unacceptable at a time when we have so many technological tools available.

The other extreme is telling your life story through the medium of the application. School administrators are busy people. Applications are extensive enough already. They are probably going to skim or speed read your information. Do they really need to know that you were Homecoming Queen or the National Pinewood Derby Champion?

Find that balance between the two extremes when answering the questions. This is where your proofreader buddy or buddies will be invaluable.

# STRATEGY 14: USE COVER LETTERS THAT DON'T GET SHREDDED

Use the same brand of quality paper for your cover letter and resume. You want to have a letter that is specifically addressed to the district, and even better - the principal with the open job. I've received letters addressed to different schools, positions I did not have on my campus, and to "Mrs. or Ms. Rische." Unfortunately, my wife was not interested in perusing them.

If you are applying for multiple jobs, still use the basic content of you letter that you cut and paste to save time. Quality paper makes me stop and at least glance at it because it will stand out from standard white computer paper. When uploading, do what you can to make sure your copy is readable. Many get lost in translation during the submission.

I always have resumes and cover letters stashed in a file. You never know when an opening will unexpectedly occur. As I shuffle through my stack of cover letters – these qualities appear consistently:

1) Some type of letterhead with the applicant's name, address, contact information (phone and email). Home or personal email, instead of using a school address if possible.

2) The date the letter was written.

3) A personal greeting to me or the title/entity listed in the job posting. I realize that can't always happen, so I get if it is "Dear Sir/Madam" or "To Whom It May Concern."

4) The current job opening for which you are applying.

5) An honest statement of your full or anticipated certification and graduation.

6) One or two relevant facts about your previous teaching, student teaching, or working with young people.

7) (Optional) An awe-inspiring experience you've had like teaching in another country or being a cast member at an amusement park.

8) A statement or fact that makes you stand out from all the other applicants.

Retired Teacher and Interviewer Mark Fredman also gives this excellent insight for a top notch cover letter:

1) Use bullet points – people are innately drawn to lists, this is a good way to emphasize the points that make you right for the job.

2) Use bold typeface where there is a particularly important word that you want the reader to focus on.

3) Develop an opening sentence which grabs the reader. It does not have to be "jokey" or funny.

4) Rather than saying you are interested in the job, put forth the theory that you are the outstanding candidate for the job.[3]

So put some quality time and effort into maximizing the space of one page for a jaw-dropping cover letter. As with everything else, go online to see some brilliant examples and potential templates to use.

# STRATEGY 15:  RESUMES THAT DON'T BECOME ORIGAMI

Here's another way I'm different than some of my colleagues – I like unique and creative resumes. Brochures, Fed Ex, and gift bags have caught my attention in the past. Again, personal preference. Those types probably drive some of peer group bonkers. I get it – you don't want it to become more about the pieces of paper than what is on them. Should you include a picture? That is your choice. However, this entire book is about what small things you can do to increase your chances of getting an interview and ultimately being hired. A small picture attached or embedded in your resume might trigger a memory with the hiring committee or the principal with an opening. Hopefully it is a positive memory.

An online search will provide you with a multitude of resume examples. Several templates are also offered where you can just plug your personal information in. Find the right medium – not too flashy, but not too boring. Use quality paper that matches your cover letter. Sounds simple, but receiving a white papered Word document combined with a light tan colored resume just doesn't give a great first impression. If possible, try to keep your resume to one page so whoever is reviewing it can get a quick snapshot of who you are. Because of extensive experiences, jobs, or certifications – you may need to use two pages, and that is fine. Be selective – I knew a teacher hiring committee would not be interested in my previous jobs as a dishwasher, pizza maker, or valet parker.

Most of us keep a physical file of resumes. I always like to have potential candidates available in case of an unexpected opening. I also hold on to high quality resumes as examples. I'm not quite sure why or for whom. Going through my file, here are the pertinent categories that seem to repeat themselves:

1) Your identity – Who you are, contact information (current email address and a cell phone number is crucial), and the address of where you are residing.

2) Job objective – One, no more than two well thought out non-cliché sentences (this can be optional if you are applying for a specific position).

3) Certifications – Everything that is applicable to your teaching position. Or other certifications that will enhance your teaching because of those experiences. Make sure to include the dates of completion or anticipated completion - especially if anything is classified as "pending".

4) Education – All the universities you have attended, degrees obtained, or hours accumulated if not completed yet.

5) Teaching and work experience, related work experiences, or volunteering.

6) Special skills – Do you speak another language, have held a unique job, play a musical instrument, or have you experienced extensive travel?

7) References – It is fine to say "available upon request". There probably isn't room to list them if you're attempting to keep your resume clear and concise. You'll turn in a list of references with your application. And finally, they might change – so you don't want them permanently plastered on your resume.

# STRATEGY 16: SHOULD I USE MY BEST FRIEND AS A REFERENCE?

Reference letters will more than likely be submitted with your application. They are also a great addition to your teaching portfolio.

It is common courtesy to ask permission before using someone as a reference. You also want to give them a reasonable amount of time to write the letter before your application submission. Some teacher candidates will attach a copy of their resume with the reference letter request to help jar memories, or possibly show some areas of involvement the writer of the letter didn't know about. Gently give them a reasonable timeline for them to have it completed.

Who should you ask for a letter? Please don't have your best friend as your number one reference. Everyone already knows that they believe you're the greatest. You want letters from those that think highly of you and your potential, will say some quality things about you, and have witnessed you in a work environment - preferably teaching. Using that as a filter, think of college professors, supervisors in your teaching/certification program, school administrators, teachers you have worked alongside with, central office personnel that know you, former non-education supervisors, and parents whose children you have taken care of.

You might be a teacher currently employed, but want to change schools or districts for the next school year. Do I tell my current supervisor? What if it doesn't work out and I'm still working at that school? Won't they hold a grudge against me?

Wow, I ask a lot of questions. Seriously though, the best advice I can give is to have open, timely, up front, and honest communication on your part. And then do everything in your power to keep a positive relationship with them while displaying a strong work ethic. You do not have to give them the specific reason for wanting a change - that is your choice. There are dozens of reasons: Your spouse might be transferring or starting a new job in a new area, you may want a shorter commute, you could be curious about working with a different subject or age group, a fresh start in a new district sounds appealing, and you just may flat out not like working where you are because of your supervisor, co-workers, stress levels, or unending challenges.

The last thing your current supervisor wants is to get a phone call or email from another school wanting to ask about you as a teaching candidate – and they knew nothing about it; especially if you put them down as a reference! It happens . . .

My final point on this subject. You want your current supervisor to give you a quality, professional reference if you desire to move on. It is natural for an interview review committee to be hesitant about a candidate that does not put their current supervisor down as a reference, or sometimes they aren't even on the application. No supervisor wants to lose a superstar employee. However, hopefully their professional desire is for every employee to be in an environment where they can thrive in and are happy. Even if it means they need to ultimately say "good-bye" to you.

# STRATEGY 17: KEEP YOUR PORTFOLIO UNDER A FOOT THICK

Seriously, sometimes I've felt like I'm looking at a family photo album featuring a historical timeline because size and thickness of an applicant's portfolio. It can be overwhelming to the interview committee if your portfolio is incredibly huge. They want to focus on asking you questions and hearing your responses. However, a portfolio can be a powerful visual tool to add emphasis to a few of your answers. Reflecting on the basics a portfolio should include would be:

1) A sample lesson plan.

2) Multiple modes of how you communicate with parents.

3) Your classroom management plan – make sure positive incentives are a part of it.

4) Student work samples – this might be an opportunity to display how you differentiate work for your lower and higher achieving students.

5) Pictures of your classroom, centers that you use, and anything unique that makes your room different.

6) Student pictures showing them engaged in a learning activity you designed.

7) Positive notes from students and parents.

Just like your cover letter and resume – you want to use eye-catching, high quality materials when you are assembling it. Keep it simple, but packed with relevant content that will entice the reader to keep on turning the pages.

Should you bring a device to show an electronic portfolio or classroom webpages? Those are usually impressive unless your presentation lasts too long. Another challenge is that your web pages have so much squeezed into it and those looking at it don't know where to focus their eyes because of all of the action going on. One final warning. Sometimes there are technical difficulties, and your electronic device won't connect to whatever server (if available) is in the interview room. When using technology, always have a back-up plan.

# STRATEGY 18: DEMO LESSON? WHAT DEMO LESSON?

Some interview committees may ask for you to give a demonstration lesson. You might be given all the information you need before the interview. Or, you may participate in that magical experience of being given everything you need at the interview – and then given a certain amount of time to create the lesson and present it to the panel. There are many variables regarding if you'll have to do a lesson or not – what job you're applying for, who is interviewing you, how much time does the committee have, if the position is highly competitive and if they want to see you in action, and is it a common practice of the district?

Let's move forward assuming you will have to give a demo. If you have the subject matter and time to prepare at home beforehand – you're off to a great start. Remember to bring all the supplies you'll need for your lesson. Also politely ask how many to prepare for so you can bring enough copies of your lesson plan and any other accompanying paperwork (bring a couple extra just in case). You probably want to avoid a wild, creative, radical lesson you've never done before. However, you also want to avoid a monotone Power Point lecture featuring font size of 12 with no images. Keep it simple, but a high quality presentation that will engage your audience. If time is limited, feel free to proclaim, "The next steps would be . . . Or, here's how I would plan to meet the needs of my high and low learners." Please don't end it with, "Well, that's about all I have." Or, "That's the end!" Let your closure be a smooth transition into somehow them demonstrating what they've learned based on your lesson. Here are a few tips on what to do if you have an "impromptu" demo lesson opportunity. Personal knowledge and the Home page from Pomerantz Career Center helped with these ideas[4]:

1) *Supplies* – They should provide you with everything you need. However, you may want to bring along a sharpie or any other comfort item just in case. Sticky notes or few index cards may also add to the learning experience if you are going to ask them

to use their thinking or write down reflections (just in case paper isn't provided). Be cautious with technology if you are relying on the internet. The server might be down, there might be challenges in making a connection, or the volume could be difficult to hear. Have a backup plan in case any of those happen. One final thought – you might panic and your mind go completely blank regarding your time limit to prepare. I've had that happen to me personally when I was interviewing for central office positions. Just grab a piece of paper and write down 5 basic thoughts about your topic to use as a skeleton framework to be filled in, which leads us to point number 2 . . . .

2) *Speech* – You want your demo lesson to be highly organized and flow smoothly - like a finely tuned speech. A basic, quality speech features an attention getting introduction, a few key points, and an action-taking/inspirational conclusion. Generate warmth with a smile and making eye contact with the committee at the start. Feel free to make occasional movement throughout the room, but don't let it distract from your presentation. Same with your hand gestures – use them for emphasizing points. Start with some type of "hook" to begin – a thought provoking statistic, a meaningful question that requires hand raising or thumbs up, a relevant statement that applies to what your lesson is going to be about, or a brief story into that leaves them hanging until you conclude it at the end. Those are just a few ideas. Then, immediately move into what today's lesson will be about - briefly touching on its real world application. Warning! Make sure your lesson aligns with what you've been given to work with – a specific section of curriculum, the learning objective, the subject or topic, or learning strand. That is one sure way for you to blow the lesson – not teaching what they asked you to teach. Squeeze in time for the participants to interact with each other, share out,

think and reflect quietly, possibly move out of their seats (even if it is standing up and sitting down to get their brains active), and creatively express your learning. You are the teacher – but the teacher's role is changing into the learning facilitator and student driven classrooms. Time will probably be an issue, so whatever you can't fit in say, "Here is the point in lesson when we would _____."

3) *Smile* – Just like you began the lesson, end it with a warm smile as you conclude. Be sensitive to using your time management skills carefully. Ask at the end, "Does anyone have any questions or need clarification on anything we went over?" More than likely it will be time for the interview questions to start, however, you might be asked details about your lesson and why you designed it that way. So be prepared for either. Don't forget to collect any type of ending reflection cards or notes that you handed out. But let them keep the copy of your plans and any learning materials you distributed. Proudly and confidently have a seat. You gave it your best. Block out any negative thoughts about "Oh, I forgot that – dang it, I messed up that section". It's over, time to move on. And if you did make a mistake, congratulations - it proves that you are a human being. Plus, now is your chance to give a dynamic interview to the committee and show them your resiliency and other talents.

# STRATEGY 19: PRACTICE QUESTIONS ARE ALL OVER THE INTERNET

That is the reason I only put a few sample questions in this book. Any online search of "Teacher Interview Questions" (or any other occupation) will provide dozens of resources and examples for you. However, after a while, you'll notice they all start to blend together. You also might be wondering: Who wrote these questions (with answers frequently provided)? Have they ever actually interviewed teacher candidates? What credentials does the writer have? Are they experienced educators? Have they stepped foot in the classroom since they graduated?

It is good to have the balance of practicing answering these sample questions without your answers sounding rehearsed with little thought put into them. As a teacher, you will have to make quick decisions and react spontaneously. You also have to carefully analyze multiple situations and come up with well thought out decisions. The interview is a tremendous opportunity to show the committee you have those qualities as a strength.

With that being said . . . Strategy 20 gives you five quality questions to ponder before your interview . . .

# STRATEGY 20: CUT THE FLUFF – KNOW THESE QUESTIONS

Thanks to "The Interview Guys" for providing the framework of these reflective questions.[5]

1) Why did you decide to become a teacher?

   *The why?* Besides the obvious - you want to impact young people and have a passion for teaching (by the way that answer has been used multiple times). Possibly talk about a teacher that impacted your life. The joy you see in a student finally "getting" what you are teaching. Positive experiences working with children in various settings.

2) Why do you want to teach at this school?

   *The why?* Because it is 5 minutes from my house, and my spouse just relocated to this area. Good reasons – but probably shouldn't be the driving force of why you are trying to get hired at this specific school.
   This is a great opportunity to share some of the research you discovered about this particular school, and how it fits the multiple talents you have to offer. Discuss how your past experiences connect with what is going on now at the school – and by adding you to the staff, the school would be adding value.

3) What can you bring to our school that makes you unique?

   *The why?* This isn't a trick question, so just be honest and straightforward with your answers. Maybe you have travel or overseas experiences that could flawlessly integrate into the classroom. Perhaps you have a unique talent that would add engagement to your lessons. Or, you may have been a part of sports or clubs and you share your willingness to continue those pursuits at a school to help benefit students.

4) What frustrates you the most in a classroom?

*The why?* "Lack of respect, lack of motivation, and lack of support" (is what you are saying in your head). Whatever your particular frustration is, try to turn it into a challenge or an obstacle you are striving to overcome. Emphasize your perseverance and the progress you have made.

This is an opportunity for the committee to see what bothers you and how you'll act when faced with it. Please don't say, "Nothing frustrates me because of my great love for children." Try to pick a fairly common situation for all teachers, and think about creative solutions. Your suggestions may not fix it, but it is movement in the right direction.

5) What is your teaching philosophy?

*The why?* This topic has somewhat been addressed in other strategies throughout the book. You might want to find a quiet place and write out your philosophy in a few sentences. This will help you clarify what your deepest beliefs are, why you want to pursue teaching as a career, and what is your broader vision for educating children? Think about how you will run your class on a daily basis, connect with your students on a deeper level, and what powerful instructional techniques you use to deliver required and relevant content.

One final piece of advice regarding interview questions. Be prepared to elaborate at any time. You may be asked for greater details, another example, or a more in-depth explanation. That will reveal if your answers are too rehearsed or not, and show how well you can articulate the subject matter at hand.

One final, final bonus piece of advice. You also need to be able to articulate sometime during the interview how you know your students learn what you are teaching. Just because you deliver content in a creative, engaging, perhaps even entertaining way – does not guarantee that any of your students "got it." What kinds of formal and informal assessments do you use?

How do you use data to drive instruction? What are the signs that you pick up on that show you need to slow down and go back and reteach?

Okay, no more final advice.

# STRATEGY 21: SHOULD I MAKE AN UNANNOUNCED VISIT?

This is a tricky question because most school administrators will give you completely different answers. They are incredibly busy people with packed schedules, unexpected emergencies, and face dozens of daily interruptions. My general advice is to stop by the schools you are interested in (dressed professionally). Tell the front office personnel you are dropping off resumes because you are interested in current or future open positions. Then, patiently wait for their response. They probably will say, "Thank you – we'll see that the appropriate person gets this." If so – smile, be gracious, and be on your way. Do not be pushy trying to have a face-to-face meeting with the administrators. As I mentioned, they are probably deeply wrapped up in some issue. The majority of the time the reason isn't that they don't want to meet with you – the problem is that they can't meet with you during that particular moment you are there.

However, here is where I'm different. If I'm not busy, in a meeting, or putting out a "fire" – I want to meet candidates that stop by. It allows me the opportunity to conduct a brief 2-5 minute screening interview, review the qualifications to see if you fit a current or potential future opening, and helps me associate a face with the piece of paper called your resume.

Several years ago I had an unexpected resignation in a difficult to fill position two weeks before school started. My brain was fried as I sat in my conference room pondering that situation, candidates I had previously interviewed, and all the other hundreds of details that go with opening school. My secretary humbly poked her head in and said, "A teacher candidate named _____ just came by, and she's dropping off resumes to see if schools have any openings." I glanced at her resume – she was completely qualified for the position I needed! I sprinted out to the parking lot and grabbed the bumper to her car as she attempted to drive off (okay, a little drama to spice up the story). Anyway, she got out and came inside. I conducted an interview. Worked with HR to make sure all her paperwork and certifications were in order. She was in a classroom ready to go for Meet The

Teacher Night. She ended up being one of the finest teachers I've hired.

Not every story like that has a fairy tale ending. Honestly, unannounced visitors drive some of my comrades' bananas – and that's completely understandable. However, it is something I like to do that can really save quite a bit of time if you're the right fit walking through the door.

# STRATEGY 22: DRESS TO IMPRESS, BUT NOT DISTRACT

The title of this strategy summarizes what your philosophy should be regarding, "What do I wear for the interview?" Fashion trends come and go – but some universal truths remain regarding how to dress for an interview, no matter how cliché they sound. For example: "Dress for the job you want, not the one that you have." Also, "I would rather overdress than underdress for a special occasion." And finally, "Don't wear any accessory that would cause people to focus more on it than you." Additionally, I found this information in my notes from one of my administrator graduate classes:

> The basic look for interviewing is conservative. Look as though you would fit in. Clothing should create an overall impression. Proper dress is almost never a reason for landing a job – but that does not make it unimportant. Improper dress is the most common reason job candidates are eliminated.[6]

During my research I came across "Resume Genius' Interview Checklist." No author or date of publication was given. Even though slightly humorous, these are valid questions to ask yourself beforehand:

1) Have you had a recent haircut or styled/combed/brushed your hair?

2) Have you taken time to organize a professional looking outfit?

3) Do you have shoes appropriate for the selected clothes?

4) Is your outfit wrinkle free and worn properly (ties, belts, collars, etc.)

5) If you have poor eyesight, are you wearing your glasses or contact lenses?

6) Have you brushed your teeth to ensure non-offensive odor projection?

7) Have you planned an appropriate amount of time to reach the location of the interview at least 15 minutes early?

8) Have you researched the company thoroughly beforehand, knowing its industry, primary products/services and business ethos?


I would add to the list: Don't walk in looking like you just came from a fun filled day at the pool. Please don't smack on gum or even have it in your mouth. Sunglasses on your head are a cool look, but not for the interview. And finally, don't have an object in your hands that you twist, play with, or use as a fidget toy. Not that I've ever seen these things happen (wink - wink), just looking out for your best interests.

A while back, a colleague and I were discussing this topic in some depth. He made what I thought was a great observation. I am supposed to be getting the very best from you in your interview. For many this is their opportunity to shine above all the competition. If that person chooses to dress too casual, careless, or even sloppy – the impression they are giving is that this is as good as it gets for their professional look. They might have an incredibly extensive, top of the line wardrobe at home. However, the perception was given (whether true or not) – this is how I'm going to look when I dress up. And also, I will be dressing down from this on a day to day basis.

I can't emphasize enough the point made earlier. The odds are extremely high that your attire likely won't get you the job – but your attire could cost you the job.

# THE INTERNAL PREP PHASE

*Unless you try to do something beyond what you've already mastered, you will never grow.*

- Ronald E. Osborn

# STRATEGY 23: YOU REALLY SIGNED UP FOR TWO INTERVIEWS

The second interview takes place at the school or location where you are applying. So what is the first interview? It is the interview that takes place in your head before the actual one. It could be a few seconds or several minutes. It could be one set of thoughts or a random series of thoughts. It could be filled with positivity, confidence, and belief in yourself. Or, you could dwell on everything that could go wrong, how nervous you feel, and the possibility that you will not get the job. Here's the kicker – you have the mental strength to have a fantastic first interview.

Much has been written on the topic of mental rehearsal. From the athletic community we are learning about the valuable benefits of envisioning – seeing pictures, hearing internal sounds, accessing feelings. Rich envisioning creates in the mind what is known as the Carpenter effect. This causes nerves, muscles, and the entire body to behave as if it has experienced an actual practice.[7]

Mental rehearsal does not take long. It's possible to rerun a rehearsal film making adjustments several times. Each time you run the film, your body responds as if you had actually been there. A caution about mental rehearsal. Sometimes we can unintentionally rehearse our anxiety and actually increase what we don't want.[8]

One final word about "two interviews" – actually it could be three or more, depending on the circumstances. The first might be an initial screening to narrow down the finalists. The second possibly could be a more extensive interview with a panel. Who knows, you may get called in for another follow up as the committee is trying to decide between you and another candidate.

No matter how many actual interviews you end up having – always have the positive, focused, calm, and confident interview rehearsed in your head first.

# STRATEGY 24: IT'S OKAY TO BE HEARING VOICES (THE GOOD ONES)

This strategy is basically Part II of Strategy 23. Maybe you've had several negative experiences during past interviews that you struggle to get out of your mind. Perhaps you were answering a question and had no idea what was coming out of your mouth. You might have even given an honest answer to a question and were met with awkward silence from the committee. We've all blown it one way or another with something that happened in the past.

The greatest advice I've read on how to overcome this challenge and learn to talk to ourselves in a positive way comes from author Jon Gordon in his book *The Power of Positive Leadership*:

Dr. James Gills accomplished the remarkable feat of completing a double triathlon (two triathlons back to back with only a 24-hour break). Even more remarkable is that Gills completed a double triathlon six times, and the last time he did it he was 59 years old. When asked how he did it, he gave the best advice I've ever heard. He said, *"I've learned to talk to myself instead of listen to myself."* He memorized scripture and would recite it to himself when he needed a boost. Gills continued, "If I listen to myself, I hear all the reasons why I should give up. I hear that I'm too tired, too old, and too weak to make it. But if I talk to myself, I can give myself the encouragement and words I need to hear to keep running and finish the race." It's the same way with life. Too often we listen to ourselves and hear all the complaints, self-doubt, fear, and negativity that lead to unhappiness, failure, and unfulfilled goals. But just because you have a negative thought doesn't mean you have to believe it. Many of you negative thoughts come from fear and the truth is that fear is a liar. I've learned that instead of listening to the negative lies, we can choose to feed ourselves with the positive truth. We can speak truth to the lies and fuel up with words, thoughts, phrases, and beliefs that give us the strength and power to overcome our challenges and create an extraordinary life, career, and team. Whatever comes your way, just keep running, stay positive, talk

40

to yourself (instead of listening to yourself), and make sure you celebrate and raise your hands in the air when you've reached your destination.[9]

# STRATEGY 25:  HOW'S MY BEHAVIOR BEEN?

If you've been a hard working student, a dependable, in-demand worker, and have a cheerful disposition – the odds are strong that you will carry those traits into your teaching job. If you are late for work and in turning things in, have an average attendance record, and are the first one to race to the parking lot and screech your tires as you leave – the odds are strong that you will eventually carry those traits into your teaching job. Many businesses and school districts use Behavior Based Interviewing. Behavior-based interviewing (BBI) comes from the business world, where it has been used successfully for at least two decades. The premise of behavior-based interviewing is that past behavior is the best predictor of future performance. BBI questions typically start with "Tell me about a time when . . .""Describe an incident where . . . "or, "How have you handled this issue in the past?"[10]

Because of the high stakes involved for schools to find the perfect fit for any open positions – screenings, applications, the interview process, and reference checks have become much more extensive. Dr. Bob Smith has written a book called *The Three Essentials*. His research and screening tools make complete sense based upon the fact that everyone acts different under stress. He declares: "When we develop an understanding about people that uses a simplistic structure, we will always be left with an approach that will not work when the pressure or stresses get high . . . People are more difficult to understand than finance, game theory, or the law. So we have to abandon the commonly used, elementary methods if we are going to improve our effectiveness in hiring, training, promoting, motivating, developing people, and building teams."[11]

So remember this insight as you work, are at home, or attend classes today. Anyone can put on good behavior for an extended period of time. However, who you truly are will eventually show up because life is filled with stress and unpredictability. Strive every day to do a little something to become a better "you".

# STRATEGY 26: THAT TRICKY "WEAKNESSES QUESTION"

Let's face it. This is the question we all dread, but we know is coming sometime during the interview: "Tell us about your weaknesses."

"Well, let's see. There are many: I am impatient. In group work – it is my way or the highway. And finally, I don't return messages to parents – they can figure out their issues on their own!"

Okay, so we need to sugarcoat this response a little. You proclaim, "I don't have any weaknesses" – then everyone knows you're fibbing. If you're brutally honest like the above statements – you'll probably bring the interview to an unexpected and abrupt early conclusion.

I was honored to hear the late Zig Ziglar speak in person many years ago. One of his famous quotes was that, "Your weaknesses are really your strengths out of balance." Think about that statement for a little while and how it could apply to your life.

*EntreLeadership* offers great advice: Be realistic and mention a small work related flaw. Many people will suggest answering this using a positive trait disguised as a flaw such as 'I'm a perfectionist' or 'I expect others to be as committed as I am.' I would advocate a certain degree of honesty and list a true weakness. Emphasize what you've done to overcome and improve. This question is all about how you perceive and evaluate yourself.[12]

This is another possible suggestion: Recall a teaching experience that went poorly. What would you do differently? New Teacher Resources claims, "We applaud people who can pinpoint what went wrong"[13] No one expects you to be perfect. The ability to look internally and make adjustments speaks volumes about your potential to continue growing.

My personal opinion, stay away from saying, "I don't enjoy conflict and try to avoid it." Besides Professional Wrestlers, most people don't enjoy conflict and want to avoid it. However, it is almost 99.9% guaranteed you will face some type of conflict as a teacher with either students, parents, guardians, co-workers, administration, central office, the pizza delivery guy – it is simply unavoidable when you're working with that many people. Maybe at one point it was a weakness - and you can share how you continue to grow, made it through some tough circumstances, and what you're doing now to make this weakness an asset or strength. If not during "the weakness question" – the odds are high that you will be asked to describe a time or two regarding how you handled conflict with someone besides your spouse, significant other, or your own kids. Do not just gloss over this question. Speak to the problem, how you addressed it and took action to fix it. What was the final result – how do things stand now? Please, please don't respond with, "I get along with everybody – I avoid drama and I am the ultimate team player."

# STRATEGY 27: WHAT IS YOUR "WOW" FACTOR?

What makes you different than the hundreds of other applicants that are seeking the same job that you are? What unique experiences or talents do you have that will benefit students and the campus you are on? Why should the committee select you?

Those are tough questions that you need to honestly sort out before the interview. Competition is fierce. Certifications and degrees are abundant. Cover letters and resumes sit in stacks resembling small towers.

The world of marketing encourages business or product owners to have an "elevator sales pitch". Meaning that if you were on an elevator for 30-60 seconds with a potential client – how would you convince them to purchase your product in that short time span? See if you can develop a pitch "selling" your teaching abilities. At job fairs, when I ask, "Why should I hire you over all the other thousands of people that are here today?" Sometimes I'm met with a blank stare and a candidate stumbling through an answer. Other times the candidate is ready, willing, and able to tell me in a condensed version why they are the best.

Along with your "wow" factor – I always encourage candidates to clarify in their head 2 or 3 items about themselves that they want to make sure and communicate before the interview ends. The worst feeling is driving home and remembering, "Dang it – I forgot to tell them that I _____!" Having those items crystal clear in your mind will allow you to depart from the interview knowing you shared what is most important to you.

# STRATEGY 28: WHAT IF MY BRAIN FREEZES DURING THE INTERVIEW?

Hopefully this won't happen. By practicing interview questions, reflecting on what makes you different than all the other candidates, and clarifying your beliefs are all proactive approaches to help prevent a mental lapse at an inappropriate time.

However, you are human. If you draw a mental block on a question, here are a few ideas to potentially get you back on track again.

1) Ask if the question could please be repeated. This gives you a little extra time to stall and jog your memory.

2) Or, you might ask a question for clarification to make sure you understand what is being asked. Again, this provides a little more time to stall.

3) Inhale a slow deep breath through your nostrils and then slowly exhale. The importance of proper breathing all throughout the interview process is discussed in Strategy 41.

4) Understand that it is okay to occasionally pause to contemplate your responses. It is an unreal expectation for you to rattle off answer after answer without sounding too rehearsed.

Eventually, you'll need to say something. Extensive awkward silence is after all . . . awkward. Sometimes when you start talking about the key words in the question – the answer you've been waiting for will all of a sudden pop into your head. Last resort if nothing absolutely doesn't come to mind – kindly ask if the interviewer would come back to the question.

# STRATEGY 29: SHOULD YOU TAKE NOTES?

My advice is that it is perfectly fine to take notes during the interview within reason. You may find it helpful to quickly jot down important information that comes up during the conversations. You could briefly write down key word questions that you want to save for an appropriate time during the interview or at the end. Maybe inconspicuously quickly transcribe the names of the committee members for a glance during the interview - or as a reference for who to send your thank you notes to afterwards.

You don't want to take notes if it is going to be any type of distraction or as a reference for answers during your interview. Continually looking to your notes for guidance while being questioned strongly portrays a potential weakness you are displaying is the inability to think on your feet. If you start scanning your notes with your finger or flipping pages – that creates an uncomfortable pause during the session – and the committee is probably thinking about the next candidate.

In summary – okay to have, but proceed with caution.

# STRATEGY 30: WHAT ABOUT EYE CONTACT?

This is still an area I'm working on when I give a public presentation. It is easy for me to fall into a lull and keep staring in the same general area, or looking at the same people. I've had to work at scanning the eyes throughout the room, every now and then locking eyes with someone like I'm speaking to them personally, and catch myself addressing objects instead of people.

If you struggle with making eye contact – the good news is that you can practice it in a variety of ways before your interview occurs. When you're in a store, carefully look at the name tag of the person serving you. Then, look them square in the eye with a smile and address them by their name. They will probably react in a surprised way. Even in your personal conversations – focus on the pupils of their eyes and actively listening to what they are saying. Our default habit is to be multi-tasking when someone is talking – or saying "uh huh" and thinking about what you are going to say next.

I've gone as far as setting up my kid's stuffed animals around a table and practiced talking to them. Be prepared to do some serious explaining if a family member walks in.

One final word of advice from Tim Wei, "Make eye contact with all the interviewers at the table, not just the principal. I've sat in on many interview committees and have noticed that many candidates look directly at the principal and seem to ignore the rest of the panel. Be sure you make eye contact with everyone at the table."[14]

With everyone, not just the person who asked the question. When practicing with stuffed animals around the table or objects it might sound something like this: "That's something I've experienced several times Mr. Teddy Bear. Last year, I had a student that . . . "

# STRATEGY 31: THOSE DREADFUL "UMS" THAT WON'T GO AWAY

For a smoother interview, it would be great to eliminate "um" and "uh" from your vocabulary. You may not even realize you have a problem with it. One evening, my gracious wife listened to a new presentation I had put together. She immediately noticed how much I was saying "um" – I wasn't even aware of it. We came up with a drill when she would lift her hand every time I said it. It is still an area I'm growing in improvement. Simply being cognizant of it is the first step in becoming a more polished communicator.

"Um" has several purposes – mostly it is used as a filler word, or we say it when we are transitioning to a different topic. If we don't know what to say or are pausing – we use it. Frequently people will be trying to talk too fast, and their sentences will unknowingly be sprinkled with "ums". Most of us are conditioned from an early age to answer questions immediately. It is natural to develop the habit of creating some type of fillers or words to fill the void until we can collect our thoughts.

The London Speaker Bureau shares some ideas to overcoming this habit by practicing telling stories in front of someone (and have them signal when you "um"), make sure you have engaging content, prepare and over prepare your presentation, practice focused and moving eye contact, and finally - record yourself with audio or video equipment to perceive as to how you come across.[15]

Another technique to practice is replacing "um" with other transition words or phrases, "Next, we're going to . . . Moving forward . . . I want to . . ." using your creativity, there is potential for endless possibilities.

One final thought from The Harvard Extension School. They recommend the mantra "Pause, Think, Answer."[16]

If these suggestions don't work . . . then, uh . . . er, um . . . I don't know what to tell you . . . .

# STRATEGY 32: POWER POSES

Author and speaker Amy Cuddy is world renowned for the work she has done in the field of using body language and non-verbal communication to build your self-confidence. She has an amazing story of overcoming a debilitating injury from a car wreck. If you have time, take a look at her book *Presence*, or watch one of her talks online for inspiration.

Ann has several recommendations to use before an interview, a crucial conversation, a presentation, talking to your boss – or anything that produces anxiety. Her reasoning is that by striking certain poses before our big moments in private – we are creating an image in our minds of us in powerful position, we literally are making ourselves bigger by physically stretching and extending ourselves, and we are fighting our natural tendencies to slouch and subconsciously have closed off body language. Don't you want that as the last image in your mind, and as a resource to draw upon if anxiety starts to mount?

Her book is filled with a multitude of simple yet effective techniques. Two of the most popular are the Wonder Woman (guys can pretend they are Superman) and the Finish Line Victory pose. For Wonder Woman, you stand with your hands on your hips, feet are shoulder width apart, and your head is held high. To perform the Finish Line, simply raise your arms up high like you'd just crossed the finish line in first place in some competition. Maintain these poses for several minutes in front of a mirror if at all possible. Smile, stand up straight and proud, chest out, and keep your chin up.[17]

I would recommend the poses before you leave your place of residence. I would also recommend quickly doing them in the restroom as your waiting for your interview. In public restrooms, I've done them in a private stall to avoid stares from others in case I'm not alone.

Give it a try. It is an energizing phenomenon to walk into a possibly anxious situation with the last image in your mind of you standing proudly, victoriously, and stretched out to enlarge yourself.

# STRATEGY 33: HOW ARE YOUR TECHNOLOGY SKILLS?

Being up to date and tech savvy is important, but more critical is how you enhance student achievement and engagement using those tools. Technology devices are a moving target. Today's state of the art equipment is in tomorrow's salvage pile. It all goes back to the filter of what is best for kids. Compare for example sports and art. You may have scored the winning touchdown in your high school championship and been carried off the field – but how do bring out the best in your athletes? Your artwork may be on display in the New York Museum of Modern Art – but can you teach a kid to love drawing, sculpture, and painting? Especially if the kid proclaims the astonishing phrase, "I hate art!" Same with technology, if you relate better to machines than people – I'm sorry to say, but there is plenty of demand for you in another field besides working with students.

You may not enjoy using technology, unfortunately it is a non-negotiable for working with students today. Not only is it a major part of their world, data driven instruction continues to be a primary driver for designing lessons and delivering content. Students will tune you out if technology isn't somehow integrated into their learning.

If you feel behind in this area – it might be a great time to take a refresher class at a local community college, service center, or a university. Another option is to have a group of young people give you a crash course. Simply ask them, "How do you like to be taught?" Be prepared for an honest, possibly eye-opening response.

# THE WAITING AREA PHASE

*The most important thing in communication is to hear, what isn't being said?*

**- Peter Drucker**

# STRATEGY 34: DRIVE THE ROUTE A DAY BEFORE

The title of this strategy says it all. You may have an extreme distance to travel, or be coming in from out of state and can't accomplish this task. That is completely understandable.

However, if you are close enough – think of the many reasons why you would do this. You want to time the drive so you allow plenty of margin to arrive early. Be on the lookout for school zones that would be active for arrival or dismissal. Any new construction sites along your path? Unexpected road and route closings? Beware of rush hour traffic on the highways with the high probability of an accident slowing everyone down. What about the four way stop that gets backed up and people don't understand taking turns in a pattern? Do you have plenty of gas in your vehicle - so you don't need to stop for a fill up and accidentally spill petroleum on your new shoes?

You want to minimize stress and anxiety the day of your interview. Doing this the day before can help. If you arrive too early – relax in your vehicle and give yourself a mental pep talk.

Try to have a phone number of the school handy as you leave for the interview. No matter how early you leave – something crazy or unexpected could occur. Just calmly call the school and explain what happened – they should be understanding and hopefully the schedule can be adjusted to accommodate the situation.

# STRATEGY 35: THE OFFICE STAFF MIGHT BE SCREENING YOU

Maybe this is a paranoid conspiracy theory – but you never know who is watching you! Did you greet the office reception staff warmly and with a smile when entering? If they initiate it – make sure you engage in exchanging pleasantries in conversation with them. They might be too busy, and simply ask you to take a seat. Or, they could be watching to see your reactions to the school, the students, and your overall personality. Whatever happens, they are getting a small snapshot as to who you are and how you interact with people. They might not say a word, or they could report to a committee member, "Wow, we really liked _____." That comment might not mean a thing to the committee, or it could be the 1% difference between you and another candidate.

Either way, this is not an opportune time to be playing around on your phone (see Strategy 37).

# STRATEGY 36: TAKE IN YOUR SURROUNDINGS

While waiting for your interview, it is the perfect opportunity to observe all the details of what is going on around you. All the much better if school is still in session – and the staff and students are present.

Think back to your research on the school you did beforehand – how does it match the current reality you are viewing right now? Did you feel a particular culture and climate as you entered the building? From your vantage point – what kind of student work is displayed? Can you get a glimpse of any interactions between adults and students? How are visitors being greeted when they enter the building, or when they call on the phone? Did you notice the campus preparing for any big events that are on their calendar? In general, does it seem people are happy to be working and attending classes there?

You'll be surprised how much you can learn just by sitting there carefully watching and listening. This is an important step as you process in your mind about being a future employee at this campus.

# STRATEGY 37: GET OFF YOUR FREAKING PHONE

Your most natural reaction while waiting for your interview is to grab your phone or whatever electronic device you have to pass the time. Surely some mindless wandering on the internet or playing a game won't do any harm – and it will also help me get my mind off how nervous I feel? Don't do it!!! Wait, let me clarify that. Don't do it!!! Can you tell this is something I feel passionate about? I would recommend leaving it in your vehicle. Here is why:

1) You should be spending the time taking your surroundings (Strategy 36), recalling in your mind all the prep work you've done beforehand, filling your head with positive thoughts, and focusing on the key points you want to make sure the interview committee hears.

2) Pulling up anything on your phone now will not benefit you in any way for your interview. More than likely your email inbox needs cleaning out. It is a 100% certainty that something negative is happening in the news locally or worldwide. You all of a sudden become jealous that your cousin is posting pictures online of their wonderful cruise in the Caribbean. Shock and confusion hit when you read about the latest celebrity couple that is getting a divorce. How can this be – they seemed so happy?

3) Do you realize that when you are seated and interacting with your phone – you subconsciously are putting yourself in a slouch position? You are leaning over to see the screen, slightly relaxing and slanting your posture downward, and possibly even straining your eyes to read the tiny print.

4) You could get a call before or during the interview. Sure, it might be something important – or it could be your kids calling to tell you the dog dug a hole by your fence and is attempting to escape.

5) Which brings me to my final point. You might be asking: What if there is a true emergency? You told me to leave my phone in the car – and all these people are frantically trying to reach me! Sure, you're right – a true emergency might occur. You do take

the risk of missing out on that immediate contact if you're phone is not on your person. Let's get real – the odds are incredibly low that a serious emergency will occur within the time that has been blocked out for your interview. However, hopefully you took some proactive measures before you left. Your kids or pets are being watched by a trustworthy source that has alternate emergency numbers to call besides yours. Would you be able to get there in time to make a difference anyway?

Again, I go back to where I started. Ask yourself: Will being on your phone right before your interview add anything of value to your mental, emotional, or physical state?

# STRATEGY 38: START THINKING ABOUT "THEY AND WE" VS. "I"

Almost every interview candidate will proclaim themselves a team player and the ultimate collaborator. However, what will your language reveal? How many answers will be all about "I did this" or "I did that"? Sometimes, it cannot be helped. However, practice rephrasing your responses something to the effect of, "My students did this _____", "Our school did that _____", "We worked together as a department to _____".

It is a positive strength to be able to take the focus off yourself, and show the great things students are doing because of your facilitator skills and processes put in place to empower them.

Think about successful public speakers. They have a mystical way of making themselves seem similar to you in some way or fashion. No one wants to hear a presenter rant and rave about "I, I, and more I". They skillfully employ "us, we, you and I" to build a connection.

# STRATEGY 39: YOUR BLADDER IS NOT YOUR FRIEND

There is an ongoing joke in my household about the "David Rische Rule" when traveling. Let me explain. My wife is an international flight attendant. Occasionally, I get to tag along on one of her trips. During one Easter, she had a layover in Paris, France. We were able to see many of the main sites with a small group of friends. We absolutely love the city, however, it does have one shortcoming. There are very few public restrooms available for use (they usually have long lines), and business owners are not eager for you to use their facilities unless you are purchasing something. I guess that on more than one occasion I proclaimed whenever a restroom was spotted, "Make sure you use the restroom, even if you don't need to – because you never know when the next one will be available." So that small group has made it a running joke to share my restroom quote in whatever city, country, or public place they are in.

What in the world does that story have to do with interviewing for a teaching position? Absolutely nothing – I just wanted to tell it. Seriously though, the worst thing imaginable is if you need to use the restroom in the middle of your interview. So you need a proactive strategy to have in place. This book is all about the details – so just roll with this one no matter how trivial it may seem.

I recommend using the restroom before you leave your place of residence. Unexpected traffic or delays could make your arrival time tight. Bring your favorite water cup or a bottle of water with you to sip on during the ride so you don't faint from dehydration. Hopefully, you'll arrive early to the school as recommended in an earlier strategy. After exchanging greetings and pleasantries with the office reception staff, kindly ask, "May I please use your restroom?" Use it again if possible. Now you're ready!

Most interview committees will offer you a bottle of water or maybe even a soft drink as you enter the room – take it! During my research I was even able to find advice regarding this subject:

While no one's ever been denied a job because they said no when offered a beverage – take one. I'm serious.

Remember, your goal is to be relaxed and comfortable so you can show the best you. And think about it: You're going to be talking. A lot. Which means you are going to regret saying, "No thanks, I'm fine." To a beverage 45 minutes into the interview after you've been talking for 29 of them.

But what's more, saying "Yes, I'd love one, thank you," is the natural thing to do. When you visit a family member or friend's house, you have no problem accepting a refreshing glass of water or whatever Grandma has available. And doing the same with the interviewers will show them that you're comfortable enough to spend 40+ a week with them. (And, hey, free drink! You might not get the job, but you got a Coke, so it's not a total loss.)[18]

Don't guzzle it like a canteen in the desert - carefully sip the beverage during your time to stay refreshed and hydrated. You want to keep it balanced with avoiding the awkward "I need to use the restroom, but we are only 10 minutes into the interview, how am I ever going to make it???"

You might think this is making a big deal out of nothing. Hey, if it is a 1% difference in you being comfortable and relaxed during your interview – then it is worth implementing as a strategy. Plus, now you have timeless advice for whenever you travel . . .

# STRATEGY 40: GET PSYCHED UP IN THE RESTROOM

This sounds kind of goofy – but it can give you a private place to practice many of the strategies mentioned in this book: smiling, upright and confident posture, briefly engage in your power poses, stretching, and taking deep breaths (Strategy 41 coming up next). Hopefully no one else is in there with you, especially someone from the interview committee.

Also, it can be a great last minute check in the mirror for your hair, make up, nothing dangling from your nose, the broccoli strands from your salad at lunch, tie or scarf straightened, shirt tucked in, etc.

# STRATEGY 41: BREATHE LIKE A NAVY SEAL

You definitely want to use deep breathing to calm yourself down before the interview. During the interview if you notice yourself talking too fast, short of breath, and your heart is racing – pause, inhale through your nose and the side of your mouth, and inconspicuously exhale from your nose and the other side of your mouth. Maybe even while a question is being asked so people aren't waiting to hear words from you. It is a quick, but effective way to lessen the pace, refocus your mind, and reduce your anxiety.

The Navy Seals have used deep breathing for many years as one of their keys to success. Whether in training or on the battlefield, Seals have to be at their sharpest mentally at all times. The majority of the time they are physically and emotionally exhausted. Mark Divine, author of *The Way of the Seal* discusses deep breathing during several portions of his book. When under stress, afraid, or surprised – we enter into fight or flight mode – and that includes not breathing properly. He states, "Before you can take control of you mind, you must first calm it down. The fastest way to calm your mind, along with your body, is through slow and controlled deep breathing . . . This settling practice helps reduce mental chatter, prevents your mind from wandering, and is generally a great boost to your self-control efforts. It will also rebalance your nervous system and reduce harmful physiological effects associated with fear and stress."[19]

A final thought on breathing to help you relax. In fact, I use this technique almost every time I'm giving a public presentation:

This is the simplest and possibly most effective relaxation technique. Just before you begin to talk, take three deep breaths. They should be full and slow, all the way down, filling the lungs. Concentrate on your breathing. Think of nothing else. Just three good, deep breaths are enough. They add oxygen to the system, distract your attention from fear, and help clear your mind.[20]

If I may emphasize one word regarding this strategy – it is *inconspicuous*. The last thing you need is the interview committee summoning the school nurse or scrambling for an AED unit because they think something is medically wrong with you. A powerful, but "keep it secret" strategy.

# STRATEGY 42: THEY ARE NOT ON YOUR SCHEDULE

This is just a gentle reminder to stay flexible. In fact, flexibility is a key component of being an educator. What better time to display it than before, during, or after your interview?

It is highly likely the interview schedule for the day may be off. Administrators have to deal with interruptions and emergencies usually on a daily basis. Several candidates might be scheduled back to back for whatever reason. Someone may be a no show – and you're asked to go in early for the interview. Your time with the committee could be shortened or extended – you need to be prepared for both.

You may have in your mind "Plan A" for how the interview will smoothly and flawlessly unfold. Hopefully it will. However, be prepared to quickly shift to "Plan B" or "Plan C" as circumstances dictate. Follow whatever cues the committee gives you.

# STRATEGY 43: LISTEN TO AND REMEMBER THEIR NAMES

One of the most common flaws we have as human beings is meeting someone, introducing ourselves, hearing their name, and completely forgetting what they just said because we truly weren't listening. Work on this before your interview. What active listening and memory tools do you need to use to improve in this area? Using mnemonic devices, repeating people's names out loud, or some type of word association with their name? Work on this also in the waiting area with the office reception staff when they greet you.

Look for the interview committee to hopefully be wearing names tags. Sometimes they will have folded name tents displaying their name and position. You may even have the privilege of being told beforehand who will be conducting the interview. Listen carefully how their first and last names are pronounced. Last tip, don't call them by their first name unless you know them, they ask you to, or you just feel such a positive vibe that it flows naturally.

# STRATEGY 44: REMEMBER TO SMILE AND SLOW DOWN

The last strategy in this section is simple advice, but so easily forgotten. At any time during the interview it is easy for your nerves to get the best of you. You start to feel your palms sweat, you feel flush, and you start to speak faster interjecting a lot of "ums".

Sometimes a smile is all it takes to slow you down and help you reorient yourself. You can also intentionally inhale and exhale slowly while the next question is being asked. Recall the advice from Strategy 31 – "Pause. Think. Answer." Frequently give yourself a gentle mental reminder to not be in a rush to get out of the room. You've earned a spot in the interview chair "hot seat". You have an incredible amount of skills, talents, experiences, and love of children to offer. Being nervous is 100% normal. What you do with that nervousness is another catalyst for what may set you apart from all the other applicants.

# THE INTERVIEW PHASE . . .

*This is your big moment!*
*You are more than prepared for this!*
*Get in there and shine!*
*You've got this!*

- **David Rische**

# THE REMEMBER & REFLECTION PHASE

*Practice without improvement is meaningless.*

- Chuck Knox

# STRATEGY 45: YOU ARE ALSO INTERVIEWING THEM

A quick note on this phase of strategies after the interview. Some of these strategies obviously come into play before you go into the interview. This was one way to break up so much content presented in the previous sections. However, as you think about in the days to come how the interview went, these are potentially categories to focus on as you grow in continuous improvement.

So how are you interviewing them? By seeking clues and ques if this is the right position for you. Is this a work environment you can envision yourself being contributing part of? Would you want to be here long term? What vibes did you pick up in the waiting area and during the interview? Would it be fun to work here?

As long as you don't overdo it, there is nothing wrong about asking some clarifying questions during the interview. The type of questions asked will let you know what the school values in a potential candidate. Another minor reliever of nervousness is when the communication is two way and you're not having to do all of the talking.

# STRATEGY 46:  UNIQUE QUESTIONS WITH A PURPOSE

These questions are from an article titled "The Top 10 Interview Questions You Need to Ask" from EntreLeadership.[21] This is bonus material that could apply to any interview. The link is listed in the back of the book in the "Works Cited" section. As mentioned previously, it isn't beneficial to enter the interview with all predetermined and practiced answers to every possible question. Those interviewing you do want to see you come up with answers on the spot. I chose four of the ten questions along with the reasoning behind it just to get you thinking in a different way.

1) What can you do to help take our company to the next level?

   *The why?*  To see if the candidate has a global perspective and a vision beyond themselves. Do they have creative solutions for continuous improvement? They might provide a suggestion that could be a company blind spot that may make an incredible difference at some point.

2) Don't name names, but can you tell me about the best boss and the worst boss you've ever had?

   *The why?*  This questions reveals what a candidate likes and doesn't like in a working environment. Comments about the "worst boss" can also lead to insight regarding – was the candidate part of the problem in this circumstance?

3) What is your personal mission statement?

   *The why?*  Most people don't have one, so this question really puts them on the spot and makes them think in the moment. Interviewers can observe how the candidate processes this question. It is also interesting to hear if what is their "big picture" purpose, and how it overall ties into their work style.

4) (My favorite) How many pennies does it take to fill this room?

*The why?* Most employers are looking for problem solvers and those that think "outside the box". What's important about this question is not the final answer number total – but what process did the candidate use to arrive at the answer? Wrong answers are "I don't know", "a lot", or laughing it off.

Just some food for thought to help stretch your brain a little. A former colleague of mine used to ask somewhere in the middle or toward the end of the interview, "What would you do if you won the lottery?" The question has absolutely nothing to do with their teaching skills – just something to break things up a little, observe their processing, and maybe even catch the candidate off guard.

# STRATEGY 47: QUESTIONS TO AVOID ASKING THEM

These are from personal experience and ideas presented in an excellent article titled "What Not to Ask in an Initial Job Interview."[22]

1) What is the starting salary?

   *The why?* In all honesty, the committee probably doesn't know what the exact salary will be. And in all honesty, salary is important because we have to eat and pay bills. The happy medium is finding the answer online, or contacting the Human Resources Department and asking them before the interview. The impression you want to leave is that you want to work with students first and foremost. Asking about salary could possibly be the 1% difference between you and the candidate that doesn't ask about it.

2) When would I be considered for a promotion, a move to administration, or central office?

   *The why?* Unless you are interviewing for one of those positions, you want to leave the committee with the impression that you are the perfect candidate for the role they are trying to fill. There is a good chance that they will be interested in hearing about your short and long term career goals, but let them be the drivers of that question. Again, focus on convincing them that you are the best candidate for their current opening.

3) Can you tell me about how many vacation days I get and the insurance package?

   *The why?* Same reasons as the salary question. Asking about vacation days and time off could trigger thoughts regarding your reliability, attendance - and is your number one desire to work with students? Insurance and benefits questions can be answered by Human Resources or possibly by someone else <u>after</u> you've been given a job offer.

4) What will I be doing every day?

*The why?* The committee needs to be assured that you are a self-starter, internally motivated, and can integrate your past experiences into this new position effectively. Hopefully, a job description is posted before the interview. If not – seek out a friend, classmate, or even contact another district for information. Then you will be able to show you have a basic foundation and understanding of what your typical day would look like.

5) Why is this job open now?

*The why?* If this topic comes up – let the committee be the one who leads that conversation. It could be that someone moved, it is a new position, or it has been added because of student growth. Or, perhaps unfortunately – the person who previously held the position was fired, laid off, couldn't get along with others, won the lottery, or left unexpectedly. This topic has the potential to be a sore subject – again, avoid it unless they want to talk about it - or until after you're hired.

One final thought about what to avoid. Probably the most popular opening conversation starter in any interview setting is the famous, "Tell me about yourself . . . " You're nervous, the interview is just starting, and you want to show that you are the person they are looking for. The default mode is to start talking about your family, hobbies, states you've lived in, pets, etc. Limit those topics to maybe one or two sentences. Remember, you're here for a teaching interview. This is a chance to bring your cover letter and resume to life. Talk **briefly** about your education, your career, and where you are currently. Start from the furthest to the present. The word "briefly" is highlighted because again, this is where the nervousness can come into play. Once you start talking, the words can start flowing effortlessly – where you lose all track of time and space. The interview panel hasn't forgotten the tight time schedule they are probably on. In conclusion, there is a fine balance between practicing your opening monologue and keeping it between 1-2 minutes – you also don't want it to sound "canned and rehearsed."

# STRATEGY 48: TOP NOTCH CLOSING QUESTIONS

Unless you are taking part in a brief screening, or the committee is incredibly short on time – you probably will be asked, "Do you have any questions for us?" Strategy 47 coached you in what not to ask. Here are some quality questions that I've either heard, or are from an article titled "Do You Have Any Questions For Me?"[23]

1) What are you looking for in a team member?
2) What technology tools are available for your students?
3) Do you have a teacher-mentoring program on campus?
4) What opportunities are available for professional development?
5) What is the school's discipline plan? (Make sure you can clearly articulate your classroom management/discipline plan).
6) How active is the PTA with the school?
7) What is your vision for the campus?

That is just a sample of questions – I wouldn't recommend asking every single one of them. They are there to help you get past your mind going blank at the end of the interview, and to help protect you from rushing out the door due to nervousness. Plus, some of these topics may have already been answered in the interview or during your investigative work beforehand.

If it isn't mentioned, you do want to politely ask, "What is the timeline for your decision?" You also want to clarify about being contacted regarding if you are the chosen candidate or not. Some databases will automatically send an email to all the applicants once a position is filled. Some principals will personally call or email the applicants. Usually a representative from Human Resources will contact the recommended candidate with an offer for employment. You don't want to be in the unpleasant position 3 months after the interview wondering if you got the job . . .

# STRATEGY 49:  DID YOU THANK THEM BY NAME?

Hopefully you've been practicing before the interview memorizing first and last names, or using nametags to personalize communication with others. As you're leaving, an authentic smile and sincere "thank you" can finalize your interview on a positive note. Sure it's time to go, another candidate is probably waiting in the foyer – but you don't want to race out the door before acknowledging those in front of you. Maybe the interview committee has nameplates displayed by their seats or they are wearing name tags. Possibly you knew beforehand who was going to be on the committee. Perhaps there was a gap during the questions, and you were able to jot down everyone's name. Time and the room setup may not allow you to physically shake each person's hand. However, you can still say thank you and goodbye with a slight wave or palm extension towards each person addressing them by name or official title as you make your way towards the door. It is a small but powerful gesture that leaves a good feeling surrounding your exit.

# STRATEGY 50: LEAVE WITH A "WIN-WIN" ATTITUDE

It is easy to drive home from the interview and immediately negative thoughts start flooding your mind: "I can't believe I said _____." Or "I can't believe I forgot to say _____." "I feel like I bombed it." We all need to stop being our harshest critics. Combat perfectionism – no one says and does everything 100% perfect. Strive for excellence instead of being perfect. You gave it your best shot – so start reprograming your mind with everything that you did and said right.

The only things you can control are your preparation and delivery. That is the primary focus of this book. You can't control who is on the committee, what tasks and questions were chosen, or the exact person they have in mind for the job. Were you prepared the best that you could be?

If you got the job, great! If not, great! That means there is something different and better for you to discover.

# STRATEGY 51: "THE RIGHT FIT" IS A TRUTHFUL STATEMENT

I have been told several times that I "wasn't the right fit" for positions I've applied for. I've also used that phrase many times when having to inform candidates that they weren't selected to be recommended for hire. Being human beings, our initial reaction can be one of disappointment, hurt feelings, or questioning – "What did I do wrong?"

A comparison can be made to parents saying "no" to a child that is requesting chocolate cake for their entire dinner. Whether it is life experiences, nutritional value, not wanting to spoil the child, knowing the sugar will hype them up, etc. The parent knows more than the child – and they have a big picture perspective of what giving in to that request will mean for everyone involved.

You might be a phenomenal, lights-out candidate, apply flawlessly every strategy in this book, and your resume is loaded with world-class experiences – but it is just not the right place at the right time. And that is perfectly okay.

Like the parents, the interview committee knows what you don't know. They might need a particular personality to balance out a team. They could be seeking a veteran or a brand new teacher to compliment a team. It possibly could be a high turnover position or high stress position - and they want to be triple sure this is the right selection. The district may have budget constraints they have to factor in their decision. A group of challenging, high needs students could be eagerly awaiting for whoever steps into the classroom doorway. I could go on endlessly with reasons why.

If this happens – accept it, briefly grieve if you need to, speak kindly regarding the interview committee, hold your chin up high – and keep moving forward in pursuit of your dream. You are the right fit for someone. You never know – the same committee could call you back for another position, they might recommend you to another school or individual, or circumstances later on could dictate that you end up being the right fit!

# STRATEGY 52: SEND A THANK YOU, BUT DON'T BE A PEST

You want to send each member of the committee a thank you. A short, hand-written (but legible) card adds a nice touch. If the decision is being made quickly or it is during summertime, then use email. Either way, make sure you get a second set of eyes to proofread whatever you have before it is sent.

At job fairs, I must admit receiving a hand written thank you note before I left for visiting with someone for a few minutes is impressive.

Then comes the tough part – waiting. And waiting some more. Don't call, badger, drop hints, contact someone who might know the results. Don't send a second or third email. Your efforts will do absolutely nothing to sway their decision. Actually, if you're too pushy – that may help them clarify to not consider you for the job.

Perhaps someone from the school will contact you needing more information or ask to set up a follow up interview. Then it is okay to break your silence and reestablish communication.

# STRATEGY 53: WHAT IF THEY WANT YOU, BUT YOU DON'T WANT THEM?

Maybe you're half way through the interview, and you have an incredible sinking feeling in your gut that this is not the right job for you. My advice is to finish the interview to the best of your ability. Or, you complete the interview – and have a message from the school five minutes from your home that they want to meet with you. Maybe you've interviewed at multiple locations, and one clearly stands out from the others. But you're waiting, and no one is calling.

Nobody but you knows your particular situation and how long you can possibly hold out for what you perceive as the perfect fit. If you receive a job offer from a school that isn't your first choice, have an open and honest conversation with them. Decline the offer if you know it is not the right fit for you. No one wants to go to work every day with regret. You want to do this in a timely manner because the school has their timeline for hiring someone - and they are probably in competition for other candidates. Remember, you want to leave a professional impression with them for possible future openings – or that they would speak highly of you to colleagues.

Carefully think about declining a job offer. Perhaps this is the opportunity for you to get your foot in the door and gain some valuable experience for a few years?

However, you must consider – what if my plans don't work out? What if my ideal situation backfires, and I go from multiple offers to zero? Can you take the risk of not having a job if your perfect scenario doesn't go as you envisioned?

# STRATEGY 54: ARE YOU WILLING TO TAKE A PAY CUT?

In spite of having the opportunity to interview, you're not getting any job offers. Maybe you aren't even getting interview appointments. Perhaps the possibilities have been extinguished regarding any teaching jobs that you are interested in.

One of the best ways to get your foot in the door and prove yourself is by becoming an educational aide or a substitute. Take an inventory. Maybe you can afford a lower salary for the time being. You might need some more on the job training and experiences in a school setting. A job with a lower time and stress commitment level could free up time for you to obtain additional certification or training.

As a substitute, you can control your schedule. In a large district, you can probably find work almost every single day classes are in session. Plus, you should take advantage of the opportunities to try different ages and subject areas to truly discover what is best for you. Become the substitute that is everyone's first choice and at the top of the call list. Or, become the educational assistant that everyone says, "You are going to be a great teacher someday." Believe me – it happens.

# STRATEGY 55: REFLECT, REGROUP, & REPEAT IF NECESSARY

One of my favorite Jon Maxwell quotes is, "Sometimes you win, sometimes you learn." Every interview is a learning experience. Your willingness to reflect, grow, and improve will give you a foundation to keep building on. Be proud of the fact that you landed an interview in the first place. Something about you stood out.

You never know what discussions went on behind closed doors. They may have wrestled with the decision, and you were possibly the second choice. The interview committee might pass your information on to a colleague with a similar opening. Your name may come up later in the year if there's an unexpected vacancy.

Keep asking yourself the tough question: Is teaching right for me? If the answer is a resounding "yes" – then keep persevering, growing, learning, volunteering, and improving. Think back to what went well during the interview. What didn't go so well? What areas can you sharpen to present a better version of who you truly are? Continue to reflect on the past to fix the future. Don't get caught up in negative thinking and feeling sorry for yourself.

The world needs what you have to offer. From little children to teenagers – students are looking for role models, inspiration, creativity, enthusiasm, hope, skills, confidence, new learning, and someone that will push them to greatness. Most importantly, they need unconditional love. Are you that person? If so, keep pressing forward until you reach your desired goal.

Please keep in touch and let me know about your interview experiences. Did a particular strategy or strategies make a major or minor difference for you? Were you able to land your ideal teaching job? I can be reached at:   david.rische@gmail.com   Thank you for letting me be a part of your journey!

# ACKNOWLEDGMENTS

With thanks to the incredible group of encouraging individuals that pushed me before, during, and after this project. Thank you: Kelly Rische, Eric Jensen, Dr. Jim Ewing (ewinglearning.com), Ken McGuire, Carrie Jackson, Heather Varon, Amber Wynn (teacherspayteachers.com/Store/To-Third-With-Love), Tammy Mack, Michelle Stone, Karin Mahlenkamp, Sarah Germany, Jacque Hughes, Lauren Sanchez (lauren@fierce45.com), Missy Morse, Kathy Mitchell, Erica Wood, Dalana Burnstad, Lyndsi Moore, Kevin Dougherty, Kristen Ericksen, Shayne Kriz, Kathy Redmond, Amy Erb, Vicki Bunn (theheightchurch.net), Claudia Hittle, Lisa Alford, Danielle Grimes, Denise Powell Stevens, Jill Kersh, Juli Maddy, Lisa Cutting, Kim Blevins, Brad Tyler, Eve Lopez, Christa Whitmire, Whitney Wheeler, Tina Molhoek, Kristi Ryan, Traci Kraeszig, Ashley Vick, and Marcy Tate.

# ABOUT THE AUTHOR

David Rische is a public educator, writer, presenter, and Bible teacher. His goals include helping people deepen their relationship with God, and strengthening their personal productivity. His other books include *Five Toughest Decisions Teens* Make and *Five Prayers That Can Change History*. David and his family live in Keller, Texas. You can follow him at www.davidrische.com.

# WORKS CITED

1) Gary Hopkins, "What Qualities Do Principals Look For In a New Teacher?," *Education World*, April 2017, PDF.

2) Mary C. Clement, *The Definitive Guide to Getting a Teaching* Job, (Maryland: Rowman & Littlefield Education, 2007), 4-5.

3) Mark Fredman, *Teaching Job Interview Secrets Guide* EBook, (available         for         purchase         at www.teachingjobinterviewsecrets.com), 22.

4) Pomerantz Career Center Homepage, "Tips for Teaching an A+ Demonstration Lesson." (no date given). https://career.uiowa.edu/tips-teaching-demonstration-lesson

5) Mike Simpson, "5 Common Teacher Interview Questions And Answers." 2017. https://theinterviewguys.com/teacher-interview-questions-and-answers/

6) Ronald Caloss – lecture notes taken from the course: *Leadership in the Instructional Setting*. 1993.

7) Robert J. Garmston and Bruce Wellman, *How to Make Presentations That Teach and Transform*, (Alexandria, VA: ASCD, 1992), 38-40.

8) Ibid., 38-40.

9) Jon Gordon, *The Power of Positive Leadership* (Hoboken: John Wiley & Sons, Inc., 2017), 52-53.

10) Mary C. Clement, *The Definitive Guide to Getting a Teaching Job*, (Maryland: Rowman & Littlefield Education, 2007), 55.

11) Bob Smith, *The Three Essentials*, (Dallas, TX: Clear Direction, Inc., 2009), 7.

12) EntreLeadership Team, "The Top 10 Interview Questions You Need to Ask." May 12, 2014, https://www.entreleadership.com/

articles/the-top-10-interview-questions-you-need. 4R Interview Questions & Answers #12

13) Lisa Feder-Feitel, *Principals Share Their Secrets: How to Impress in an Interview* (https://www.scholastic.com/teachers/articles/teaching-content/principals-share-their-secrets-how-impress-interview/

14) Tim Wei, "10 Secrets to a Perfect Teaching Interview". (no date given). http://www.teachinginterview.com/article6.html

15) "11 Killer Tips to Stop Saying Um Forever". (no date given) www.londonspeakerbureau.com.

16) https://www.extension.harvard.edu/inside-extension/tips-public-speaking-eliminating-dreaded-um.

17) Amy Cuddy, *Presence* (New York: Little, Brown, and Company, 2015), pg. 279 and also various portions from the entire book.

18) Mitch Fortner, "5 Secrets for Acing Your Next Interview". 2017. https://www.themuse.com/advice/5-secrets-for-acing-your-next-interview.

19) Mark Divine, *The Way of the Seal* (White Plains: A Readers Digest Book, 2013), 34-35.

20) Robert J. Garmston and Bruce Wellman, *How to Make Presentations That Teach and Transform*, (Alexandria, VA: ASCD, 1992), 38.

21) EntreLeadership Team, "The Top 10 Interview Questions You Need to Ask." May 12, 2014, https://www.entreleadership.com/

articles/the-top-10-interview-questions-you-need.

22) Kathy Caprino, "What Not to Ask in an Initial Job Interview. April 8, 2017. https://www.forbes.com/sites/kathycaprino/2017/08/17/what-not-to-ask-in-an-initial-job-interview/#191903f85dc7

23) Mike Simpson, "Top 10 Teacher Interview Questions and Answers." 2017. https://theinterviewguys.com/teacher-interview-questions-and-answers/

Made in the USA
San Bernardino, CA
26 January 2020